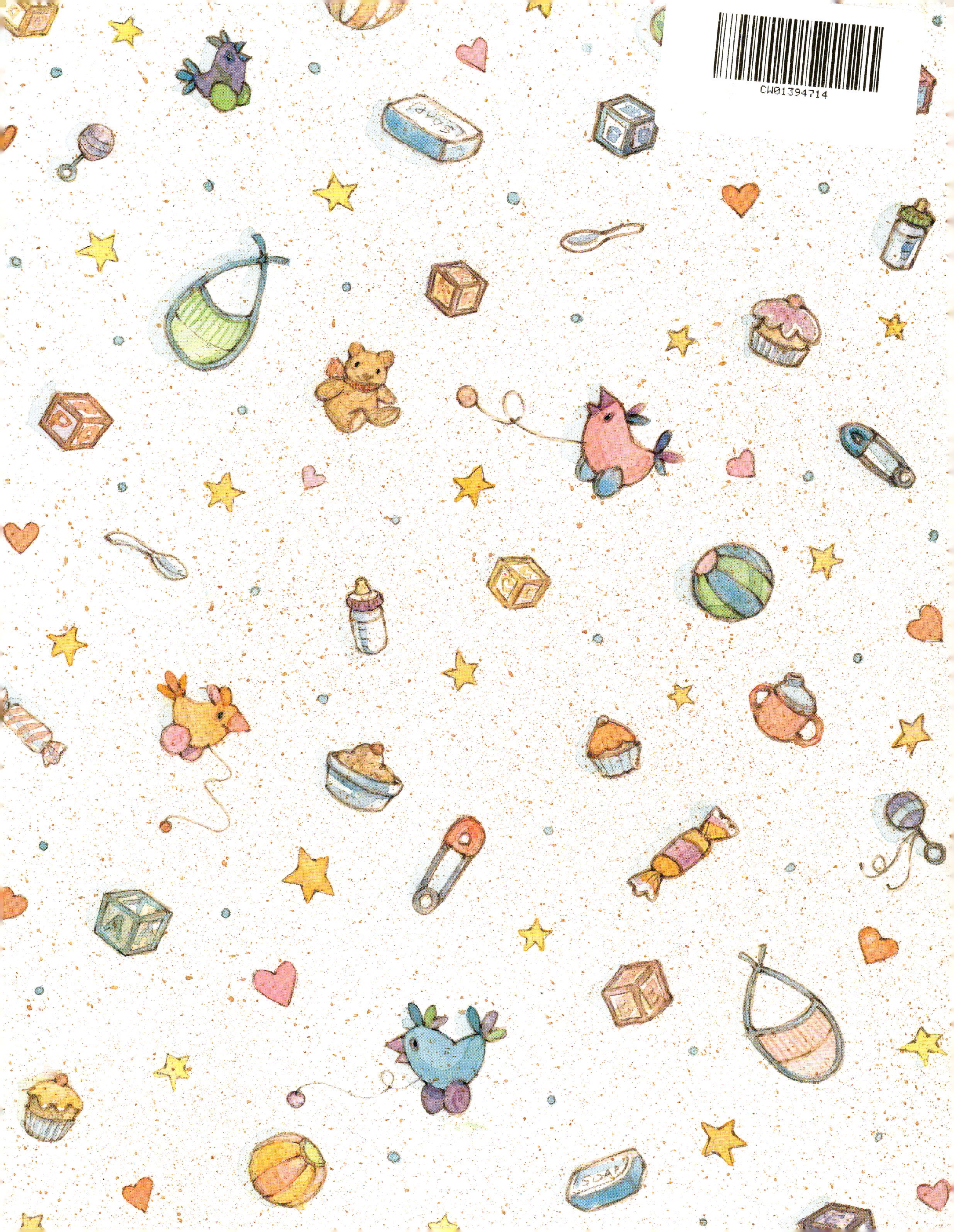
SOAP
SOAP

Sons [and daughters] are a heritage from the Lord,
children a reward from him.
Psalm 127:3 NIV

As I Remember ...my first years ©1993 **World Bible Publishers**
Iowa Falls, Iowa

Illustrated by Angela Jarecki
Edited by Glenda Hayes
Illustrations © 1993 Kingdom Resources Incorporated

Printed in Hong Kong.

As I Remember

Illustrated by Angela Jarecki
Edited by Glenda Hayes

...my first years

My name

...a book of remembrance was written before him for them that feared the Lord...
Malachi 3:16

Prenatal

Date pregnancy
was confirmed:

My doctor's name:

Visit

   Predicted due date:

   First check-up:

   First heartbeat heard:

   First movement felt:

   Special notes:

My parents' reaction to the news:

Psalm 139:13-16 NIV
    For you created my inmost being;
you knit me together in my mother's
womb. I praise you because I am
fearfully and wonderfully made; your
works are wonderful, I know that full
well. My frame was not hidden from
you when I was made in the secret
place...your eyes saw my unformed
body. All the days ordained for me were
written in your book before one of them
came to be.

My Birth Day

Birth date:

Day of week:

Time:

Birthplace:

Weight:

Length:

Color of eyes:

Hair color:

Distinctive characteristics:

Who I first resembled:

Doctor:

Nurse:

Midwife:

How we got to the hospital:

Others who were present at the time of my birth:

What my parents said and felt when I was born:

1 Samuel 1:27 & 28
    For this child I prayed; and the Lord hath given me my petition which I asked of him: Therefore also I have lent him to the Lord; as long as he liveth he shall be lent to the Lord....

Birth Mementos

Ecclesiastes 3:1-2a
   To every thing there is a season, and a time to every purpose under the heaven: a time to be born...

Birth announcement:

Birthstone: Flower:

Hospital I.D.:

My first photograph:

Footprints, handprints and lock of hair:

My Birth Certificate

My Mom and Dad

Mom   Dad

Name:

Nickname:

Birthdate:

Birthplace:

Schools attended:

Where and when Mom and Dad met:

Marriage date: Place:

Special notes:

My Name

My full name:

My nickname:

Meaning and origin of my name:

Why my name was chosen:

Proverbs 22:1
   A good name is rather to be chosen than great riches, and loving favor rather than silver and gold.

My Family Tree

Mother's birthday:

Father's birthday:

Nicknames:

Marriage date:

Pictures of how my parents looked when I was born:

_____   _____

_____   _____

My Grandparents   My Grandparents

_____   _____

My Dad   My Mom

_____

Me

My Siblings

1. _____

2. _____

3. _____

4. _____

Deuteronomy 7:9
   Know therefore that the Lord thy God, He is God, the faithful God, which keepeth covenant and mercy with them that love him and keep his commandments to a thousand generations.

Celebrations

At the hospital

　　Visitors and friencs:

Showers & parties at home

　　Hosts, dates and guests:

Romans 12:15a NIV
Rejoice with those who rejoice...

Special gifts

Who and what:

Dedication

Our church:

The ceremony

Date:

Minister:

Godparents:

Family:

Friends:

Scripture shared:

Prayers offered:

Thoughts to be remembered:

Luke 18:16
But Jesus called them unto him and said, "Suffer little children to come unto me, and forbid them not; for of such is the kingdom of God."

My First Home

Day and date of my arrival home:

My first address:

With whom and how we arrived:

Description of nursery:

Psalm 84:3 NIV.
   Even the sparrow has found a home, and the swallow a nest for herself, where she may have her young,
a place near your altar, O Lord Almighty, my King and my God.

My Firsts

My first

Bath at home:

Outing from home:

Visit to church:

Smile:

Laugh:

Tooth:

Words:

Steps:

Haircut:

The first time I

Held up my head:

Slept through the night:

Reached for objects:

Transferred objects:

Rolled over:

Ate solid food:

Sat alone:

Crawled:

Stood alone:

Walked:

Was potty trained:

My Memorable Moments

Discoveries:

Family times:

Something cute I said or did:

Psalm 33:11 NIV
   But the plans of the Lord stand firm forever, the purposes of his heart through all generations.

Memorable Pictures

My Favorite Things

Food:

Toys:

Games:

People:

Psalm 8:2a NIV
From the lips of children and infants you have ordained praise...

My Least Favorite Things

Food:

Toys:

Games:

My Growth Charts

Height – First Year

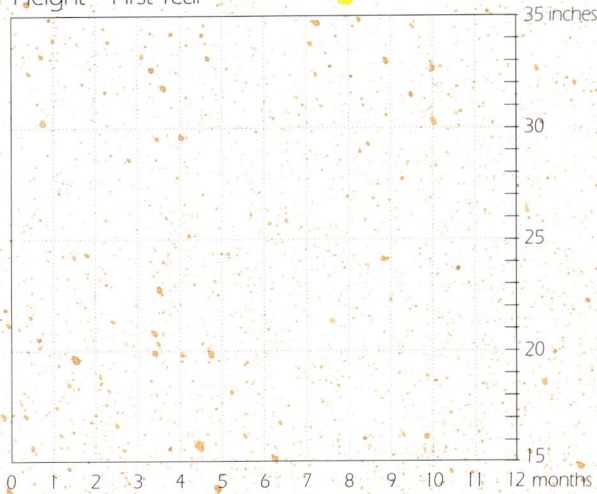

35 inches

30

25

20

15

0 1 2 3 4 5 6 7 8 9 10 11 12 months

Height – Years 1–5

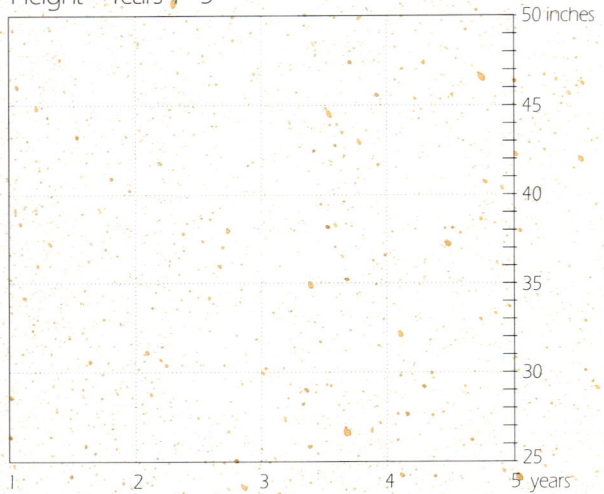

50 inches

45

40

35

30

25

1 2 3 4 5 years

Luke 2:40 NIV
   And the child grew and became strong; he was filled with wisdom, and the grace of God was upon him.

6 mo.

2 mo.

Weight – First Year

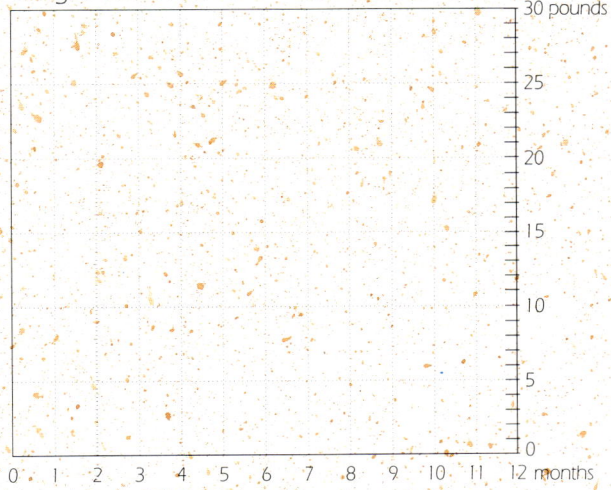

30 pounds
25
20
15
10
5
0

0 1 2 3 4 5 6 7 8 9 10 11 12 months

Weight – Years 1–5

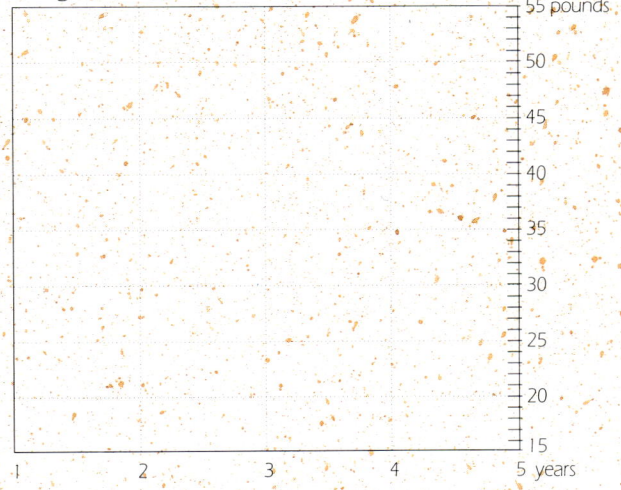

55 pounds
50
45
40
35
30
25
20
15

1   2   3   4   5 years

New habits:

New skills:

New experiences:

New favorite things:

Medical Records

My blood type:

Immunizations

Type: Date: Doctor: Reaction:

Illnesses and treatments:

Proverbs 4:22 NIV
   [For the words of God] ...are life to those who find them and health to a man's whole body.

My Check-ups

Date: Age: Doctor: Results:

My Baby Teeth

Date my teeth came in:

		left	right
A	Central incisor	_____	_____
B	Lateral incisor	_____	_____
C	Cuspid	_____	_____
D	First molar	_____	_____
E	Second molar	_____	_____
F	First permanent molar	_____	_____
G	First permanent molar	_____	_____
H	Second molar	_____	_____
I	First molar	_____	_____
J	Cuspid	_____	_____
K	Lateral incisor	_____	_____
L	Central incisor	_____	_____

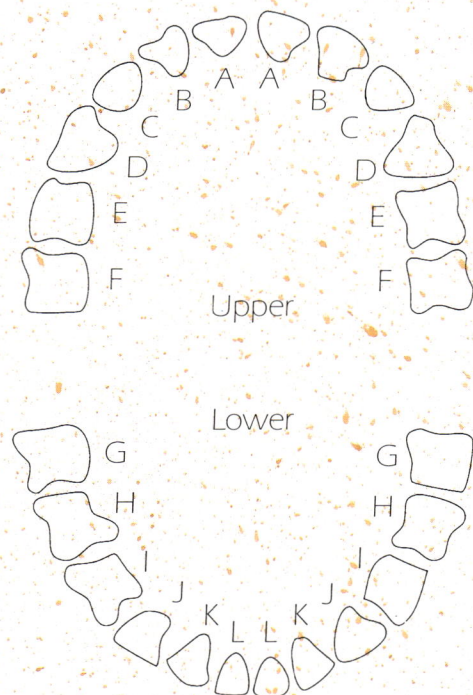

Upper

Lower

My Travels & Outings

My first car trip

Who took me:

Where we went:

How I liked it:

Things I said or did:

Proverbs 3:23 NIV
Then you will go on your way in safety, and your foot will not stumble.

My first boat ride

      Who took me:

      Where we went:

      How I liked it:

      Things I said or did:

My first airplane ride

      Who took me:

      Where we went:

      How I liked it:

      Things I said or did:

My first train ride

      Who took me:

      Where we went:

      How I liked it:

      Things I said or did:

My first camp-out

      Who took me:

      Where we went:

      How I liked it:

      Things I said or did:

My First Birthday

How we celebrated:

Who was there:

My cake:

The presents I received:

Pictures:

Proverbs 9:11
   For by me your days shall be multiplied, and the years of your life shall be increased.

My First Christmas

"O come let us adore Him, Christ the Lord..."

How we celebrated Christmas Eve:

How we celebrated Christmas Day:

Friends who celebrated with us:

Special gifts:

Other Holidays

Valentine's Day:

Easter:

Mother's Day:

Father's Day:

Thanksgiving:

Exodus 10:9 NIV
"We will go with our young and old, with our sons and daughters...because we are to celebrate a festival to the Lord".

Preschool

Where I went to preschool:

My teacher's name:

Friends:

Proverbs 22:6

Train up a child in the way he should go: and when he is old, he will not depart from it.

My School Days

First grade

    Where I went to school:

    My favorite teachers:

    My best friends:

    My favorite subjects:

    My picture:

Second grade

    Where I went to school:

    My favorite teachers:

    My best friends:

    My favorite subjects:

    My picture:

Proverbs 23:19 NIV
   Listen, my son, and be wise, and keep
your heart on the right path.

Third grade

        Where I went to school:

        My favorite teachers:

        My best friends:

        My favorite subjects:

        My picture:

Fourth grade

        Where I went to school:

        My favorite teachers:

        My best friends:

        My favorite subjects:

        My picture:

My Friends

My favorite pictures of my friends and me:

Proverbs 18:24
A man who has friends must show himself friendly: and there is a friend that sticks closer than a brother.

I Ask About God

Memorable Spiritual Moments

Psalm 33:1-5 NIV
Sing joyfully to the Lord, you righteous; it is fitting for the upright to praise him. Praise the Lord with the harp; make music to him on the ten-stringed lyre. Sing to him a new song; play skillfully, and shout for joy. For the word of the Lord is right and true; he is faithful in all he does. The Lord loves righteousness and justice; the earth is full of his unfailing love.

My Parents' Prayer

John 17:26a NIV
I have made you known to them, and will continue to make you known in order that the love you have for me may be in them...

Notes

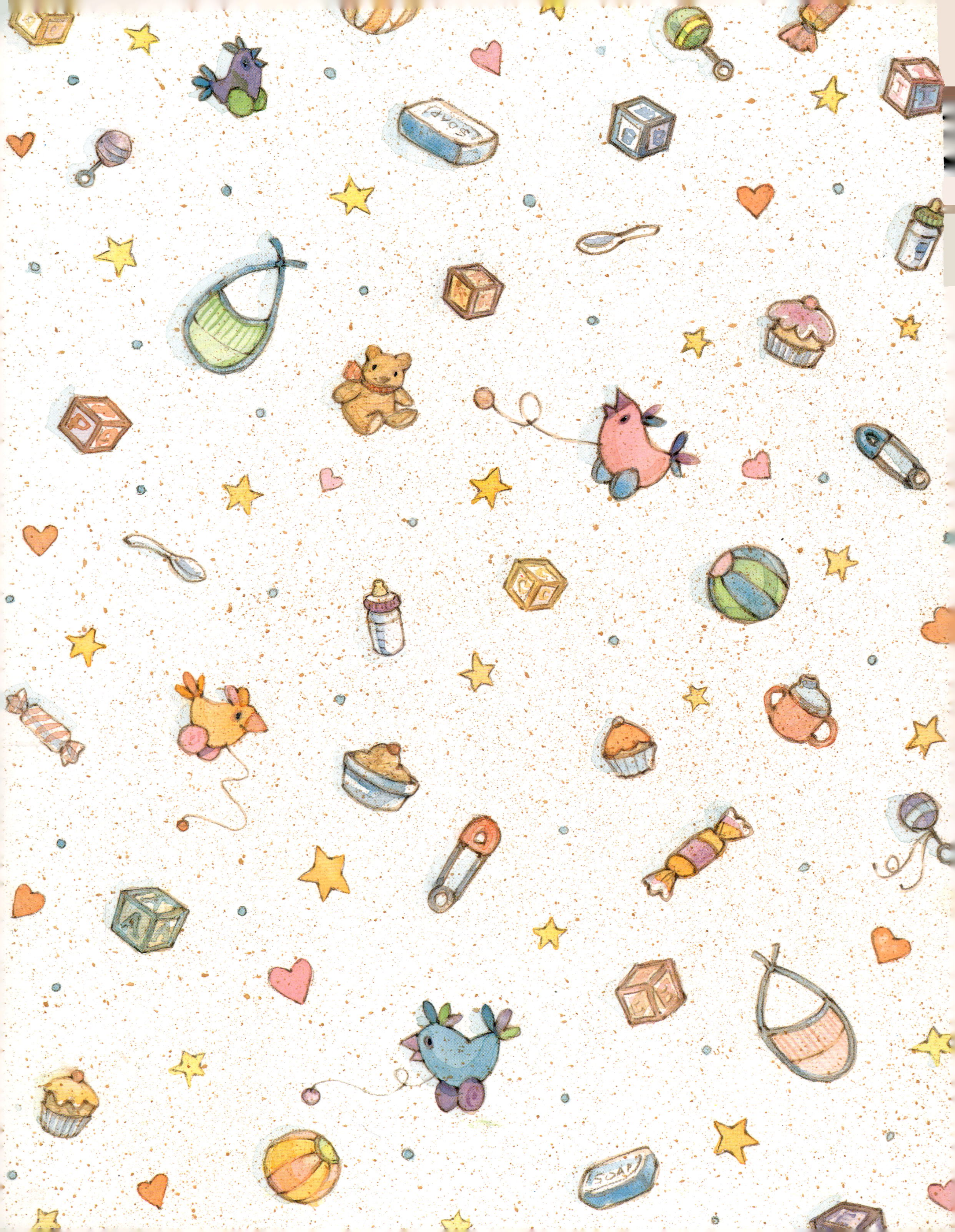
SOAP